anythinl

D0535215

A Pet

The Sound of P

By Alice K. Flanagan

I took my pack.

3

I put my pack on my back.

5

I went to find
a pet.

I met a pet on the path.

I met a pet
in a pen.

I met a pet
at the pond.

13

14

I picked the pet as my pal.

He jumped into my pack.

17

My pet makes me happy.

My pal and I
are friends.

21

Word List:

happy	pen
jumped	pet
pack	picked
pal	pond
path	put

Note to Parents and Educators

The books in this series are based on current research, which supports the idea that our brains are pattern-detectors rather than rules-appliers. This means children learn to read easier when they are taught the familiar spelling patterns found in English. As children encounter more complex words, they have greater success in figuring out these words by using the spelling patterns.

Throughout the series, the texts provide the reader with the opportunity to practice and apply knowledge of the sounds in natural language. The books introduce sounds using familiar onsets and *rimes*, or spelling patterns, for reinforcement.

For example, the word *cat* might be used to present the short "a" sound, with the letter *c* being the onset and "_at" being the rime. This approach provides practice and reinforcement of the short "a" sound, as there are many familiar words made with the "_at" rime.

The stories and accompanying photographs in this series are based on time-honored concepts in children's literature: well-written, engaging texts and colorful, high-quality photographs combine to produce books that children want to read again and again.

Dr. Peg Ballard
Minnesota State University, Mankato

The Child's World®
childsworld.com

Published by The Child's World®
1980 Lookout Drive • Mankato, MN 56003-1705
800-599-READ • www.childsworld.com

ACKNOWLEDGMENTS
The Child's World®: Mary Swensen, Publishing Director
The Design Lab: Design
Michael Miller: Editing

PHOTO CREDITS
© Albert Pego/Shutterstock.com: 6; aldegonde/
Shutterstock.com: 5, 18; Artush/Shutterstock.com:
cover; Erni/Shutterstock.com: 13; iko/Shutterstock.com:
17; InBetweentheBlinks/Shutterstock.com: 9; Ivonne
Wierink/Shutterstock.com: 14; Koldunov/Shutterstock.
com: 10; kolessl/Shutterstock.com: 21; Winai Tepsuttinun/
Shutterstock.com: 2

ISBN 9781503809109
LCCN 2015958484

Printed in the United States of America
Mankato, MN
June, 2016
PA02310

ABOUT THE AUTHOR

Alice K. Flanagan lives with her
husband in Chicago, Illinois, and
writes books for children and teachers.
Ever since she was a young girl, Ms.
Flanagan has enjoyed writing. Today,
she has more than 70 books published
on a wide variety of topics. Some of
the books she has written include
biographies of U.S. presidents and first
ladies; biographies of people working
in our neighborhoods; phonics books
for beginning readers; informational
books about birds; and career
education in the classroom.